A Note from the Author

Inspired by my 6 nieces and nephews, along with time spent studying and working as a Marine biologist, I created the "Animal Stories" series, with its bright, colourful pictures, child friendly words and scientifically accurate information, I hope everyone enjoys exploring the underwater world with Whitney and her friends.

Jon

Note to Parents, Guardians, Nursery Nurses, Teachers and Other Professionals

The Animal Stories series of books has been written and illustrated with a variety of special educational needs in mind;

• The font used throughout the books is "Dyslexie" and has been specially created to aid people with dyslexia to read easier, faster and with fewer mistakes.

• The repetition of words and phrases along with the language used is intended to help new readers recognise words and aid reading.

• The bold colours and simple illustrations, combined with the limited number of words per page and relatively short stories are designed to keep the interest of those with short attention spans like ADHD sufferers

Alongside all of the above, the simple biologically accurate stories and "The Biology Bit" at the end of each book, are designed to spark interest in the natural world and its ongoing conservation and protection for future generations to enjoy.

Whitney the
Whale Shark

Written and illustrated
by Jon Adams

This is **Whitney the Whale Shark**,
Whitney lives in the warm tropical
oceans around the world.

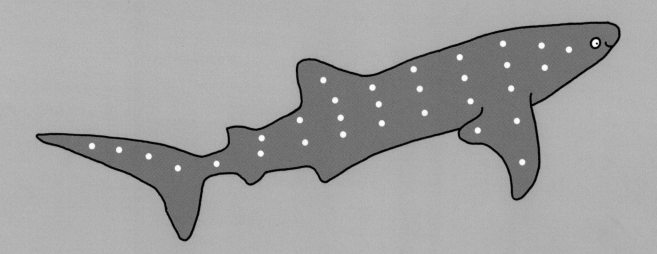

There are lots of different types of sharks, like...

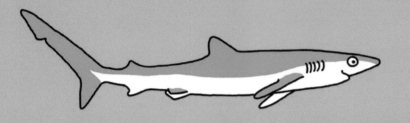 Blue Sharks...

Goblin Sharks...

 and Cat Sharks.

Whitney is a Whale Shark, the biggest fish in the whole ocean, and eats tiny animals called plankton.

One day Whitney was swimming looking for food and she got trapped in a fishermans net!

Whitney thought, "Oh no! I am trapped! Some people like eating shark fins, they might try and eat mine!" Whitney struggled to get free, she struggled and struggled and struggled.

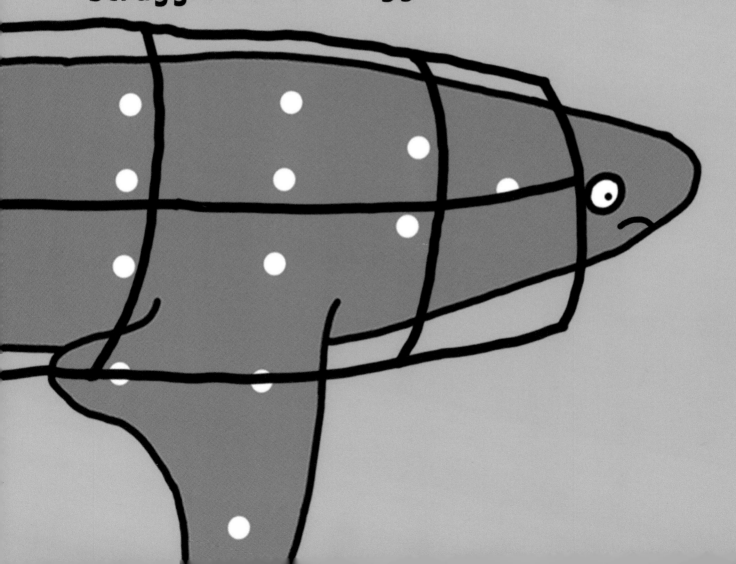

Just as Whitney was about to give up
Timmy the Turtle swam past.
Whitney said, "Please help me Timmy,
I have got stuck in a fishermans net,
some people might try and eat my
fins!"

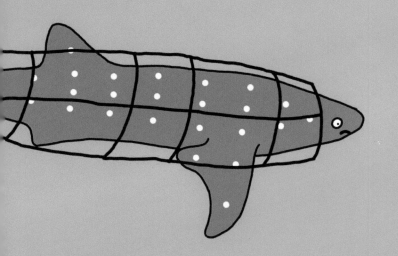

Timmy said, "I am not going to help you, you are a shark and sharks eat turtles like me".

Whitney said, "No Timmy I am a Whale Shark, not a Tiger Shark, I only eat tiny plankton".

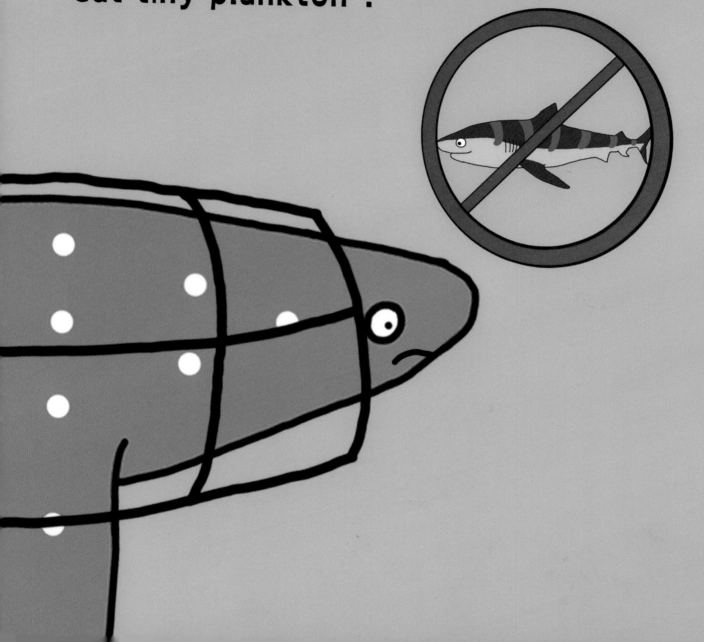

Timmy said, "I do not believe you, plankton are tiny and you are massive!" Timmy swam away as fast as he could.

Whitney said, "Why does everyone think I want to eat them? Do they not know there are different kinds of sharks?"

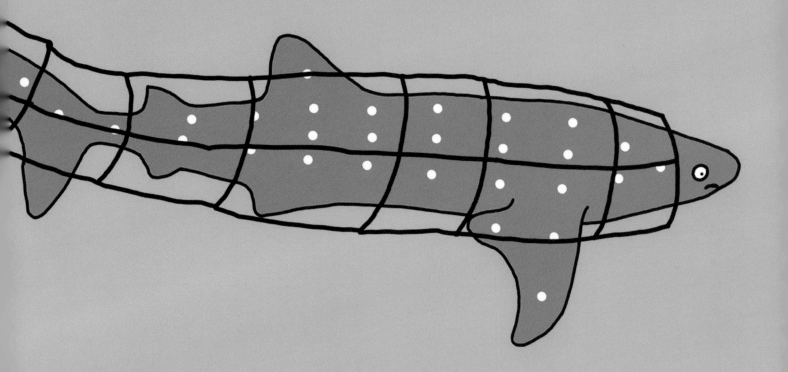

Just then Sacha the Sealion came swimming past, Whitney said, "Please help me Sacha, I have got stuck in a fishermans net, some people might try and eat my fins!"

Sacha said, "I am not going to help you, you are a shark and sharks eat sealions like me".

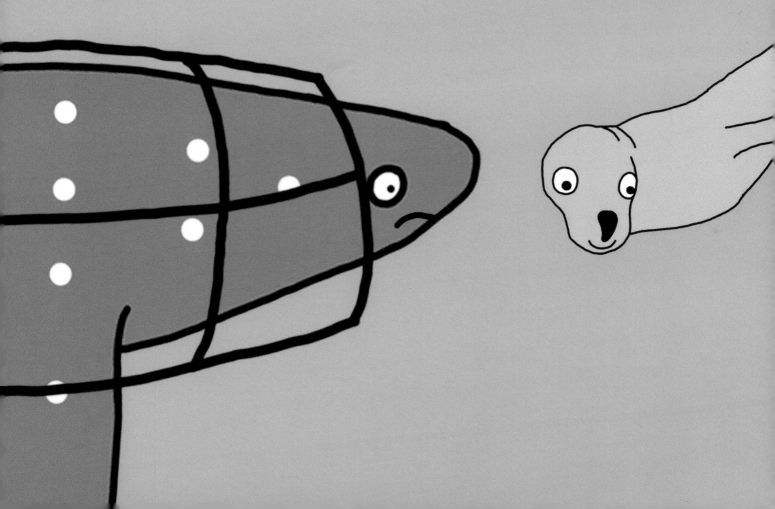

Whitney said, "No Sacha I am a Whale Shark, not a Great White Shark, I only eat tiny plankton".

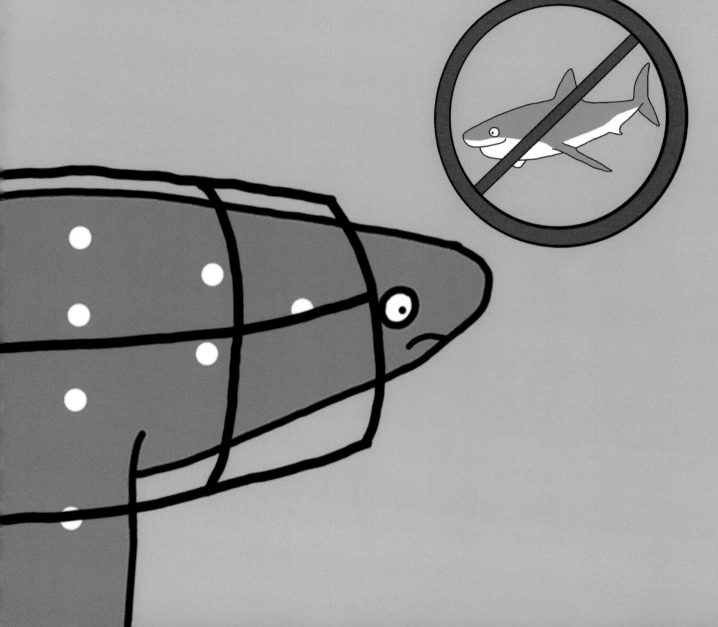

Sacha said, "I do not believe you, plankton are tiny and you are massive!" Sacha swam away as fast as she could.

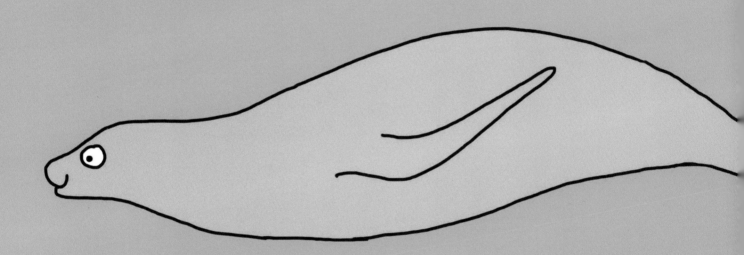

Whitney said, "Why does everyone think I want to eat them? Do they not know there are different kinds of sharks?"

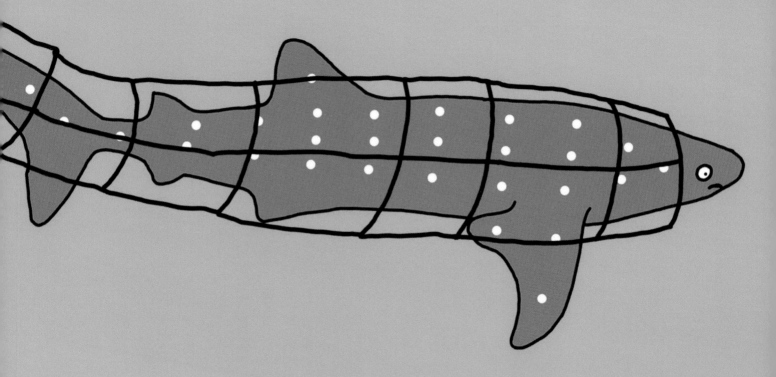

Just then Reggie the Ray came swimming past, Whitney said, "Please help me Reggie, I have got stuck in a fishermans net, some people might try and eat my fins!"

Reggie said, "I am not going to help you, you are a shark and sharks eat rays like me".

Whitney said, "No Reggie I am a Whale Shark, not a Hammerhead Shark, I only eat tiny plankton".

Reggie said, "I do not believe you, plankton are tiny and you are massive!" Reggie swam away as fast as he could.

Whitney said, "Why does everyone think I want to eat them? Do they not know there are different kinds of sharks?"

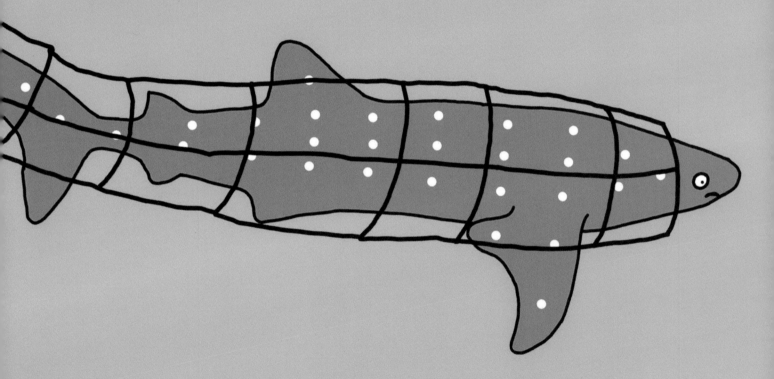

Just then Jack the Jellyfish came swimming past, Whitney said, "Please help me Jack, I have got stuck in a fishermans net, some people might try and eat my fins!"

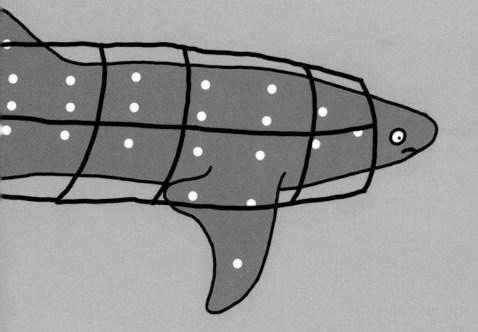

Jack said, "I know some sharks eat jellyfish, but I also know there are different kinds of sharks, and I do not think you are a type that will eat me. I am going to help you".

Timmy, Sacha and Reggie all shouted,
"No Jack, she will eat us!"

Jack ignored the other animals and
started to untie the fishermans net.

After a long time Whitney was free and said, "Thank you so much Jack, I am glad you knew not all sharks want to eat everybody", and she swam off to find some tiny plankton to eat.

The End.

The Biology Bit

• All the animals found in "Whitney the Whale Shark" are based on animals found in the tropical seas around Mexico and the south western United States of America. The characters are limited to family groups not individual species as many animal families (like crabs) share characteristics across the globe meaning the same characters can be used across the Animal Stories series.

• Whitney the Whale Shark is a Whale Shark (Rhincodon typus), the largest fish in the sea Whale Sharks feed almost exclusively on the smallest animals in the sea (plankton), these rare sharks, like most shark species, have been extensively fished so their fins can be used to make shark fin soup.

• Timmy the Turtle is a Green Turtle (Chelonia mydas), not many predators can scare a mature turtle, however the jaws of the tiger shark (Galeocerdo cuvier) combined with their persistence could mean the end for even the thickest shelled turtle.

• Sacha the Sealion is a Californian Sealion (Zalophus californianus), part of the pinniped family (seals, sealions and walrus) the sealions agility, flexibility and speed are their main defence against most predators, the Great White Shark (Carcharodon carcharias) has learnt that with a bit of planning and patience and more than a little luck, even sealion can be on the menu at certain times of the year.

• Reggie the Ray is a Smooth Sting Ray (Dasyatis brevicaudata). Most animals wouldn't try and eat a sting ray, the few that would have trouble spotting the rays if they bury themselves under the sand. With a wide head packed full of sensors that detect muscle movements, and a natural immunity to the sting ray venom the scalloped hammer head shark (Sphyrna lewini) is a sting ray specialist.

The Biology Bit

• Jack the Jellyfish is a Moon Jellyfish (Aurelia aurita). Not many things bother to eat jellyfish as they have no bones or internal organs to speak of and offer very little nutrition. Of all the animals in the story, "Jack the Jellyfish" should worry most about "Timmy the Turtle" as many turtle species will happily eat the odd jellyfish given the chance.

• Without doubt the biggest threat to all shark species today is the shark fin soup industry. Considered a delicacy in some parts of the world the fins of sharks are added to soup to give the soup a jelly like consistency, the fins themselves do not add any flavour to the soup and the same effect can be created using gelatine.

Also Available.

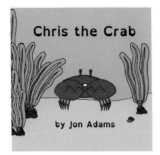

Chris the Crab
by Jon Adams

Tina the Tang
by Jon Adams

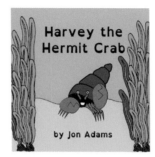

Harvey the Hermit Crab
by Jon Adams

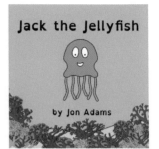

Jack the Jellyfish
by Jon Adams

Lena the Lionfish
by Jon Adams

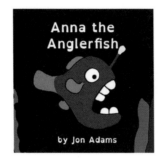

Anna the Anglerfish
by Jon Adams

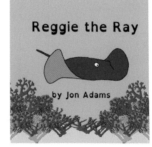

Reggie the Ray
by Jon Adams

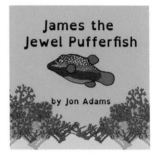

James the Jewel Pufferfish
by Jon Adams

Bo the Beluga Whale
by Jon Adams

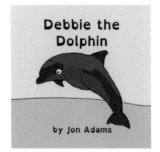

Debbie the Dolphin
by Jon Adams

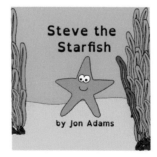

Steve the Starfish
by Jon Adams

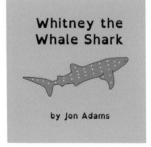

Whitney the Whale Shark
by Jon Adams

Visit www.Animal-Stories.co.uk for the latest on the Sea Stories Series.

Printed in Great Britain
by Amazon